Effects of

MW01697650

by Lorrie Oestreicher

PEARSON
Scott Foresman
DK

How does technology affect our lives?

New Challenges

We use technology all the time in everyday life. **Technology** is the knowledge, processes, and products that we use to solve problems and make our work easier. Technology makes our lives more comfortable and healthy. It helps us get the things we need.

Technology affects all living things. Sometimes technology's effects are unplanned. These effects can be harmful to living things. Motor vehicle emissions, industrial wastes, and insecticides are some of these unplanned, harmful effects. The United States and other countries must deal with air, soil, water, and noise pollution.

Technology has changed the way we do our jobs. It has helped make work easier. Machines can produce more and do work faster than people can. Unfortunately, this can lead to people losing their jobs. Although technology can cause problems, at the same time it can also help to solve them. Some machines can do work that is too dangerous for people to do. New technology can also bring new jobs. Many of these jobs are in the electronics industry.

Technology may lead to more cities that look like this one.

Technology and Materials

This in-line skater is using many products of technology. The materials in the equipment are not all found in nature. Many were made through technology. The in-line skates and protective gear are made from plastic, metal, rubber, and nylon. Some of these materials come mostly from natural resources. Others come from materials that have been made from natural resources.

Iron ore is a natural resource. It is used to make steel. You can find steel in the wheel bearings, screws, and axles of in-line skates. The plastic materials are made from chemicals. All of the plastic parts are shaped into the different pieces of equipment. Even clothing can be made from chemicals or recycled plastic materials.

Helmets are light, but they have a hard outer shell. This helps protect the head from injuries.

Polyurethane comes from chemical technology. The wheels of in-line skates are often made of this material.

Technology Keeps Us Healthy

Technology helps produce new equipment. It also helps us stay safe and healthy. The gear worn by the in-line skater can absorb some of the impact of a fall. The helmet can help protect his head from an injury. The plastic cushions in the knee and elbow pads and in the wrist guards can help protect his arms and legs.

Controlling Waste

When products are made, waste and pollution are also made. Some companies are trying to make products from materials that can break down and become part of nature again. Not all materials break down easily. Products that are made through technology often will not break down easily. Products such as plastic, glass, and aluminum should be recycled. Then they can be reused to make new products.

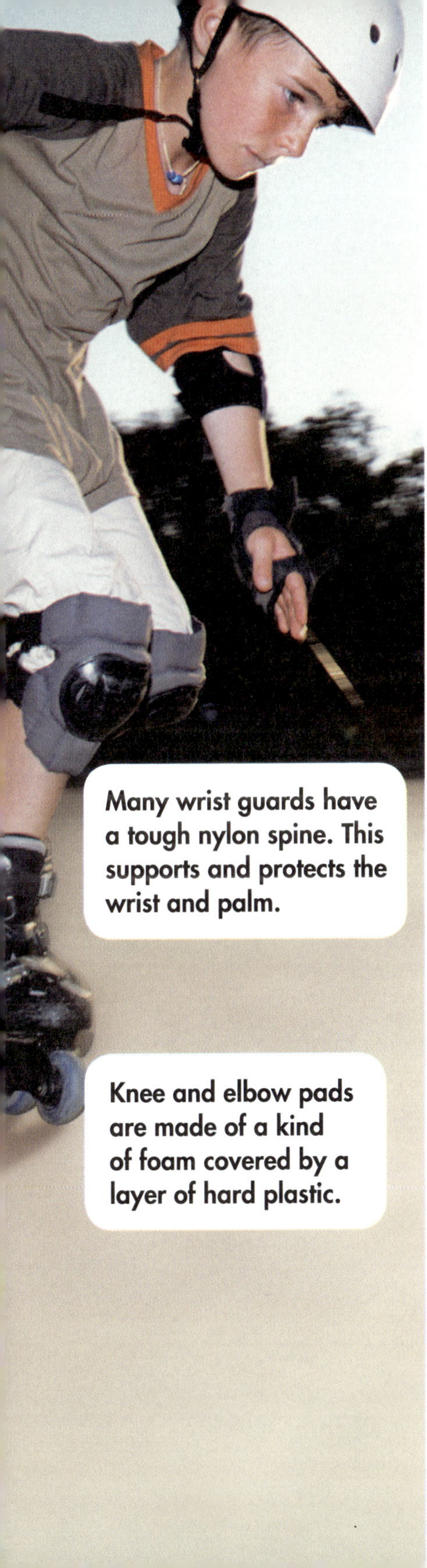

Many wrist guards have a tough nylon spine. This supports and protects the wrist and palm.

Knee and elbow pads are made of a kind of foam covered by a layer of hard plastic.

Technology and Medicine

Medical technology has changed the tools and instruments that doctors use. These changes improve the care people receive. Doctors may now use lasers in operations instead of using sharp knives. Lasers can open up clogged arteries. They can even fix broken blood vessels.

Doctors also use **optical fibers.** These are thin tubes that let light pass through them. Cameras with optical fibers help doctors see inside the body. This helps doctors decide the best way to treat a problem.

Keyhole surgery has reduced the pain and recovery time of many surgeries. With this type of surgery, doctors make only a cut about the size of a keyhole.

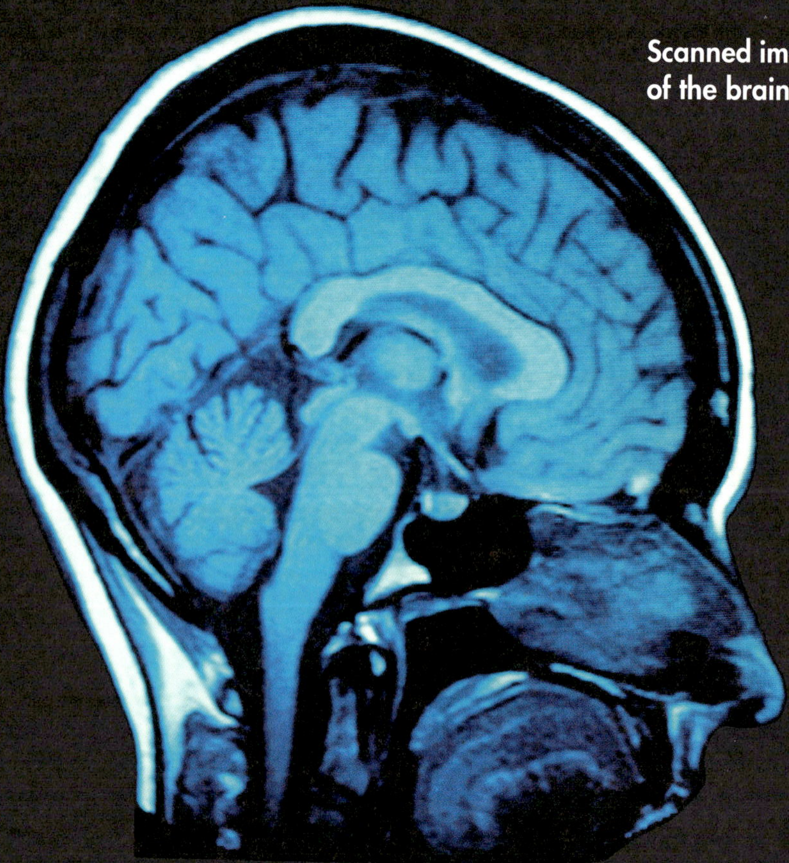

Scanned image of the brain

Technology and Food

To be healthy, you must make good food choices. We get our food from nature. To grow bigger and better crops, farmers use tractors, chemical fertilizers, and pesticides. By using these things, farmers can produce more. The crops they harvest provide the foods we need to be healthy. But the technology causes a problem if the pesticides and fertilizers harm the environment.

X rays and More

Machines also help doctors know more about our bodies. The technology of the X-ray machine allows doctors to see inside our bodies. A broken bone is easier to fix once it is seen in an X ray. The X ray shows the doctor exactly where the break is and how the bone is broken.

Wilhelm Roentgen discovered X rays in 1895. At first he did not know what he had discovered. In science, the letter *X* represents the unknown. Roentgen called what he found X rays. This was the first time doctors could see inside the body without even touching it.

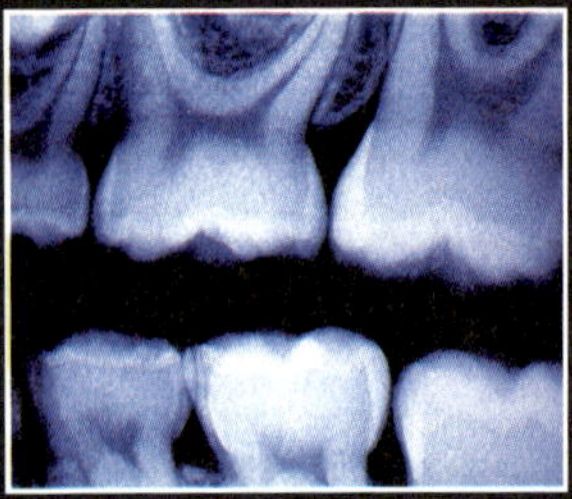

How X Rays Work

X rays pass through skin and other organs. Bones, metal, and other objects block the rays and cast clear shadows on film. We call the shadow picture an X ray.

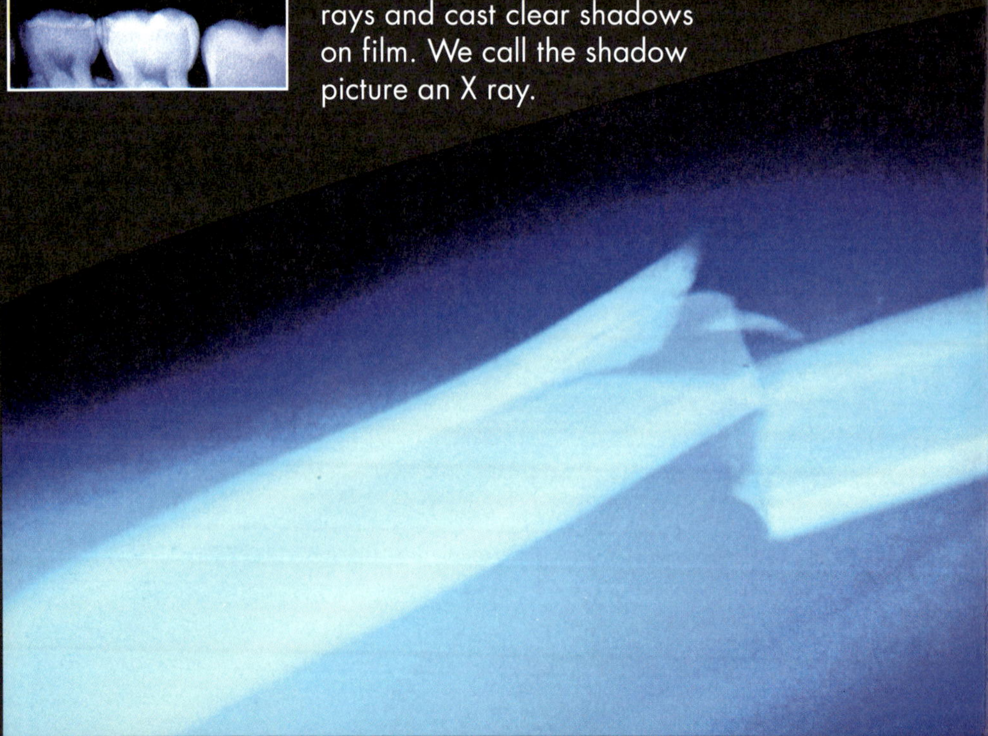

Dentists use X rays to help them find where a cavity may form in our teeth. X rays are also used to find tumors or help treat cancer. But too much contact with X rays can cause burns It can even cause cancer.

Nuclear magnetic resonance, or NMR, is a technology that helps doctors find the chemical makeup of matter. Magnetic resonance imaging, or MRI, allows doctors to see things in our bodies that X rays don't show. This technology helps doctors give their patients better treatment.

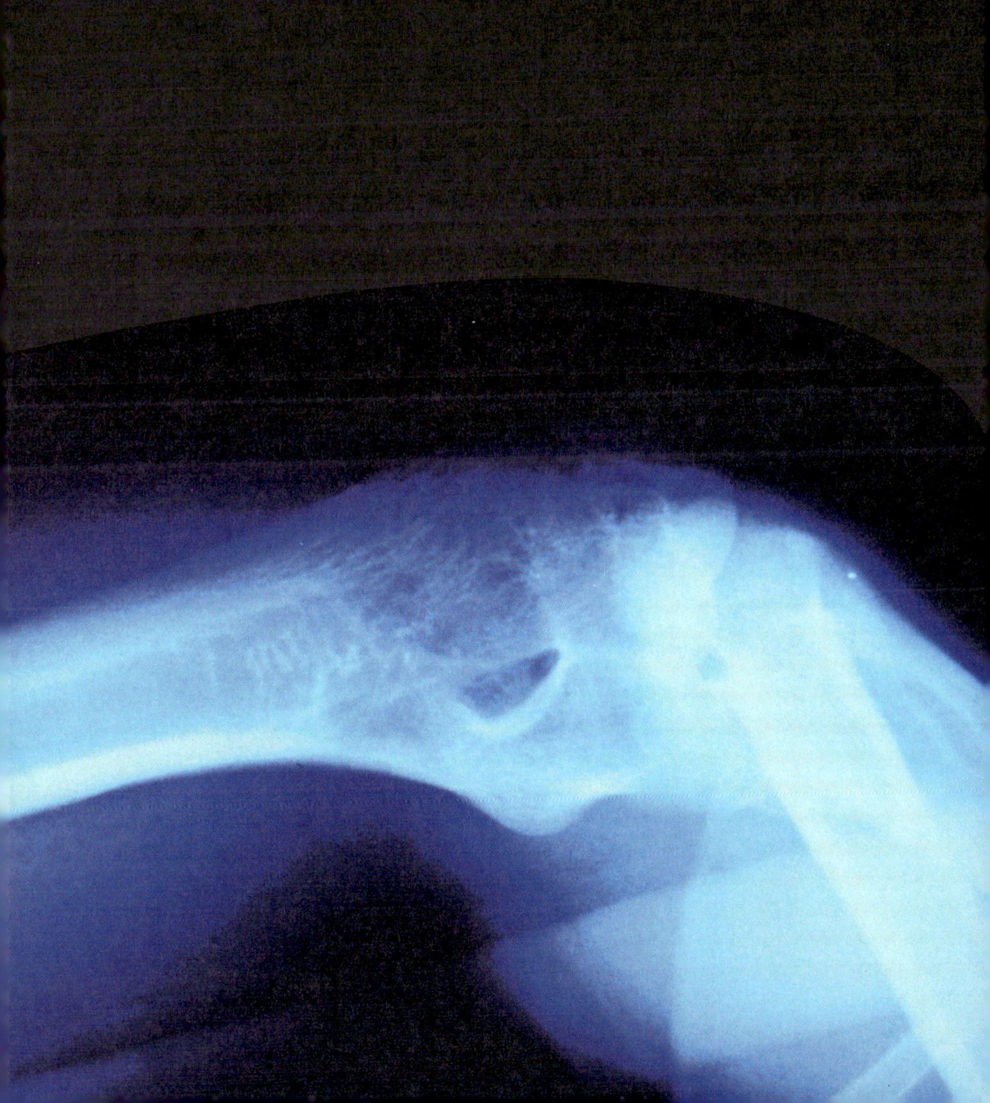

How has technology changed communication and transportation?

Communication

You are communicating any time you call someone, send a letter, or write an email. **Communication** is the process of sending any kind of message from one place to another. Communication helps you let others know what you need or what you are doing. Speaking and writing are two ways you can communicate.

Three things must happen in communication. You must send a message. The message must be received. Then it must be understood. Email is a form of communication. Letters send messages using ink and paper. Phones send messages using speech.

The quill is the hollow part of a feather. Quills were first used as pens around A.D. 600.

By 1455, Johannes Gutenberg had invented a system of making movable type with single letters.

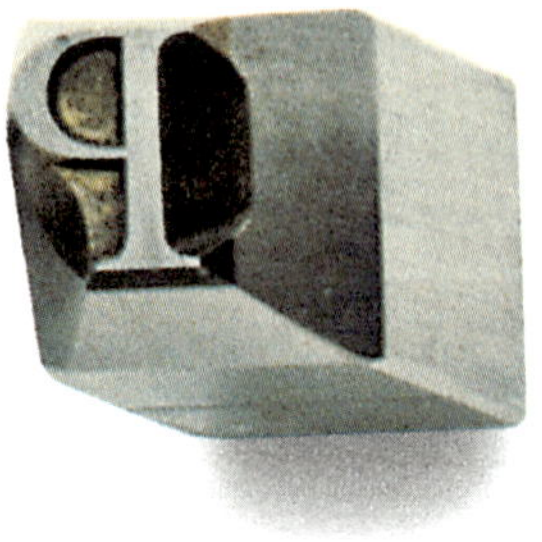

Telecommunications

Electricity changed the technology of communication. With electricity, messages could be received in seconds rather than days or weeks. With new developments, people on different continents could talk to each other. Today, technology allows messages to reach hundreds of people almost instantly.

Telecommunications are communications that are done electronically. A signal with information is sent out through a transmitter. The signal reaches a receiver. The receiver changes the signal back to a clear message. Telephone, radio, TV, and other signals are sent from one part of the world to another by communication satellites. Information from satellites helps ships, cars, trucks, and aircraft find their way.

The electric telegraph was the earliest means of telecommunication. An electric current moved through a wire in short and long bursts. These bursts were the letters of the Morse code.

A ._	J .___	S ...	2 ..___
B _...	K _._	T _	3 ...__
C _._.	L ._..	U .._	4 ...._
D _..	M __	V ..._	5 .....
E .	N _.	W .__	6 _....
F .._.	O ___	X _.._	7 __...
G __.	P .__.	Y _.__	8 ___..
H	Q __._	Z __..	9 ____.
I ..	R ._.	1 .____	0 _____

Transportation Systems

People and products move from one place to another using transportation systems. The people and goods are often carried in a **vehicle.** A vehicle may be a car, truck, train, ship, plane, or even a rocket. Vehicles travel on roadways, railways, waterways, and through airways. Today it may take just a few hours to make a trip that once took days or even weeks.

Engineers are always looking for new technology that will make vehicles safer. Seat belts, air bags, and bumpers make cars safer. But the cost of each improvement can raise the price of the vehicle.

1807: Robert Fulton builds the *Clermont.* It is the first steamboat that carries passengers—and stays in business.

1869: The transcontinental railroad across the United States links the East and the West. The railroad is completed at Promontory, Utah. The last spike is made of gold.

1903: Bicycle makers Orville and Wilbur Wright build a powered airplane. Orville flies 120 feet in 12 seconds.

Elevators, escalators, and conveyor belts also move people and goods. People design, build, run, and use these systems.

Today, computer technology often controls transportation systems. Computers keep systems running on time. They also keep the systems running properly. Space transportation uses computers and computer models. Scientists are able to solve problems such as weightlessness and airlessness from far away.

1914: Henry Ford's factory mass produces automobiles. More people can afford to own a car.

1959: Transcontinental jet service connects New York City and Los Angeles.

1964: High-speed electric "bullet trains" begin operating in Japan.

2004: In Shanghai, China, the world's first commercial maglev rail system begins operating.

The Technology of Time Measurement

Time can be measured in units such as seconds, minutes, days, and weeks. In a factory, how long do parts take to move through an assembly line? How long does it take to cross an ocean? How long does a truck take to move goods from one place to another?

Keeping track of time is important. Long ago, astronomers used the movement of the Sun to tell time. Later, people invented machines to do this. Today's clocks and watches measure time in seconds or even fractions of a second.

Many people wear watches so they know the time. The hands on a watch show the hours, the minutes, and the seconds.

New developments in technology have changed the way we live. Medical technology has improved the care doctors are able to give. Manufacturing technology has changed how products are made. Technology has changed the jobs that we do today. It has made our lives and jobs easier. Technology has improved the way people and things get from one place to another. It has increased the amount and kinds of food we grow. But, technology has also caused problems that people didn't expect. Perhaps new technology can solve these problems too.

Technology has brought us many new products. This could be the car of the future!

Glossary

communication	the process of sending any kind of message from one place to another
optical fibers	thin tubes that allow light to pass through
technology	the knowledge, processes, and products that we use to help solve our problems and make our work easier
telecommunications	communications that are done electronically
vehicle	an object that carries passengers, goods, or equipment